The Origin and the Meaning of the Name California

Calafia the Queen of the Island of California, Title Page of Las Sergas

George Davidson

Alpha Editions

This edition published in 2019

ISBN : 9789353604370

Design and Setting By
Alpha Editions
email - alphaedis@gmail.com

Vol. VI., Part I.   1910   Series II.

TRANSACTIONS

AND

PROCEEDINGS

OF

The Geographical Society of the Pacific

CONTENTS

THE ORIGIN AND MEANING OF THE
NAME CALIFORNIA

CALAFIA THE QUEEN OF THE ISLAND OF CALIFORNIA

Th⁝   to Non-Members $1.00

Pr⁝   ⁝UNCIL

The Origin and the Meaning of the Name California

Calafia the Queen of the Island of California

Title Page of Las Sergas

GEORGE DAVIDSON, Ph.D., Sc.D., LL.D.

President Geographical Society of the Pacific

Transactions and Proceedings of the Geographical Society
of the Pacific

VOLUME VI, PART I; SERIES II.

1910

Geographical Society of the Pacific

OFFICIAL DEPOSITORY ON THE PACIFIC COAST
FOR ALL CHARTS ISSUED BY THE
U. S. GEOLOGICAL SURVEY, WASHINGTON, D. C.

ORGANIZED MARCH 1, 1881
INCORPORATED JANUARY 6TH, 1892.

OFFICERS

PRESIDENT:
PROFESSOR GEORGE DAVIDSON, Ph. D., Sc.D., LL. D.
(University of California)

VICE-PRESIDENT:
HON. RALPH C. HARRISON.

DIRECTORS:
PROF. GEO. DAVIDSON,   JOHN PARTRIDGE,
HARRY DURBROW,   HENRY LUND,

TREASURER:
HARRY DURBROW.

FOREIGN CORRESPONDING SECRETARY:
HENRY LUND.
(Consul for Sweden and Norway)

HOME CORRESPONDING SECRETARY:
E. J. MOLERA.

RECORDING SECRETARY:
JOHN PARTRIDGE.

COUNCIL:
HENRY J. CROCKER,   EUSEBIO J. MOLERA,
HON. RALPH C. HARRISON,   HON. GEO. C. PERKINS,
WILLIAM HOOD, C. E.,   (U. S. Senate)
C. FREDERICK KOHL,   HON. A. P. WILLIAMS.

The Origin and the Meaning of the Name California.

Calafia the Queen of the Island of California.

Title Page of Las Sergas.

GEORGE DAVIDSON.

CONTENTS.

		PAGE
1.	*Introductory*	1
2.	*Application of the name California from Robert Dudley, 1630–47, to the authorities of the year 1903*	3
3.	*Some early charts upon which the name California is found. The First Vessel with the name California*	9
4.	*Early Spanish mention of the name California in Narratives and Documents*	17
5.	*The first mention of the origin of the name California in recent years*	21
6.	*The Causes which gave rise to the Romances*	23
7.	*The Historian Ticknor's estimate of the Romance of Amadis de Gaula*	25
8.	*Bernal Diaz, one of the Conquistadores and Historian of the Exploits of Cortes, had read the Amadis de Gaula*	27
9.	*The Mythical Amazons, the Griffins and the Terrestrial Paradise*	28
10.	*The Griffins of the Romances*	31
11.	*The Terrestrial Paradise*	32
12.	*The Origin and the meaning of the names California, Calafia, and the associated names in Las Sergas de Esplandian*	33
13.	*Translations from Las Sergas concerning the Island of California and Calafia, the Queen thereof*	35
14.	*Brief Notice of Bernal Diaz and his History of the Conquest of Mexico*	46

INTRODUCTORY.

Before the acquisition of California from Mexico, 1848, there had been several attempts to declare the origin and the meaning of the name CALIFORNIA, and in subsequent years the subject was revived. The proposed solutions indicate that the matter has not been so fully or so clearly presented to our people as it might be; and therefore we have undertaken the task of tracing the history of the name, and have ventured to give a meaning to this and associated names.

For this purpose we present such of the modern explanations as we have access to, from Robert Dudley, 1630-47, to authorities as late as 1903.

We exhibit the use of the name in early charts and in early Spanish documents and narratives to the end of the seventeenth century.

The first recent historian to point to the source of the name was George Ticknor, in his "History of Spanish Literature".

His mention of the source carries us beyond the time of the Conquistadores of Mexico, and suggests they were readers of the Romances of the fifteenth and sixteenth centuries.

This necessarily causes us to remark upon the origin, object, and character of those Romances; and upon the machinery which their authors employed.

Even when the name California is traced to its first appearance in the "Exploits of Esplandian," there is no explanation offered about its origin; but from the statement of the nominal author that this Romance was originally written in Greek, we suggest a solution.

At the close we present a free translation of parts of the text wherein "LA MUY ESFORZADA REINA CALAFIA, SENORA DE LA GRAN ISLA CALIFORNIA," plays a spectacular role in assisting the Turks in their attempt to conquer Constantinople from the Christians, with her hosts of Amazons, her fleets and her griffins.

We have descriptions of their island home which abounded in gold and precious stones, the character of the Amazons, their manners and customs, their war trappings and their animals.

We briefly relate the personal encounters of the queen Calafia with the Christian knights, her being eventually overmatched, the fury of her lionhearted sister Liota, and finally the marriage of both to Christian knights.

All these creations of the romancer conspired to inflame the younger Spanish nobles after the expulsion of the Moors and Jews from Spain, when there were no more provinces to conquer unless Columbus should discover a western route to India.

APPLICATION OF THE NAME CALIFORNIA FROM DUD-
LEY TO THE AUTHORITIES OF THE
YEAR 1903.

Robert Dudley in his "Arcano del Mare" *describes, in volume III, the chart XXXIII entitled "Il Mare d'America Occidentale"; and in speaking of the galleons from the Philippines making the northwest coast of America, says that little faith is placed on the accuracy of location of the ports on account of the notable differences of distances on the more common charts which make for example the distance between California and Cape San Lucas twelve hundred English leagues [che fanno la distanza fra la California, e'l capo s. Lucar leghe 1200 Inglese], instead of six hundred.

The last paragraph of the volume is: "The Vermilion Sea begins "at the Cape Santa Clara of California [capo santa Clara della "California], as shown elsewhere, and passes by the island which is "named de'Giganti, and is in the Northern Sea, in 43° of latitude, "through the kingdom of Coromedo; and this determines that "California may be an island off Western America and not terra "firma as [Giovanni] Jansonio states on his chart. With this state-"ment is ended the sixth and last volume. Il fino." †

In Father Bisselius' work he first mentions California on page 400,‡ where he proposes to name all the regions of the eastern and northern part of North America with the western kingdoms of Quivira and Tolmum, *Estotilandia*, and then turning to the south, on the west coast, he begins with *California*. Page 400; 337 old. ***
"The kingdoms and regions better known to our navigation are "these: those which lie on the south sea, Zurium, in an oblique di-"rection from the west; in these after Quivira and the lands of the "Tolmi, in the same extent of coast, the regions of *California* are

---

*Dell Arcano Del Mare, di Rvberto Dvdleo Dvca di Northvmbria * * * in Firenze * * * Royal Folio. 3 Vols., 1630, 1646, 1647. With charts, etc.

†Identification of Sir Francis Drake's anchorage on the Coast of California. * * * Davidson * * * California Historical Society, 1890: Page 50 n.

‡"Joannis Bisselii e Societate Iesu Argonauticon Americanorum sive Historiæ periculorum Petri de Victoria ac sociorum eius." Libri XV., M. DC. XLVII.

There were two editions. The one we have quoted is the larger, 486 pages and 12 of index with small map; the older one has 405 pages and 17 pages of index: San Francisco Free Public Library. [Destroyed in the fire of 1906.]

"stretched out on the sea toward the east, (orientem versus). The
"back of this land is shut in by mountains from which flows into the
"ocean the river Farrellónes. The sides are surrounded by waters
"in the manner of arms. On the right indeed, which looks toward
"the south, the South Sea; on the left however, toward the north, it is
"bordered by a certain gulf running transversely up beyond the
"middle of the length of *California*. Some call this the Vermilion
"Sea." *** Page 401; 33S old.

On page 402 Bisselius alludes to the numberless streams that
plunge into the Pacific from the coast range of mountains, beginning at the mouth of the [gulf of] *California*, to Nicaragua. And
further he refers to the *Gulf of California* (Californiani Sinus) and
the uninhabited islands (Desertas Insulas), as they are called.
Page 402; 339 old.

Where is the river 'Farrellones' of Bisselius? It may be the Colorado, but very likely the Rio Grande de Santiago, which breaks
through the coast range of mountains, drains the lake Chapala two
hundred and fifty miles to the southeast, and in its course receives
four or five large tributaries from the northeast and north. It
comes upon the coast at San Blas in latitude 21° 32′, longitude 105°
16′. Directly off this small port lie the Tres Marias, at a distance of
sixty nautical miles, and they rise from 1350 to 2020 feet above the
sea. They are quite large, and stretch through twenty-five miles on
a northwest course. They are covered with cedar.

George Horn, in his work on the origin of the people of America,
undertook to trace the origin and migration of peoples by similarity
of words; and writing of Corea thus curtly refers to the derivation of
the name California from the name of the Coreans: "Hi Coreani
"primo in Californiam venerunt; quae nomen suum a *Caoli* habet."
Page 243, chapter VI.

On page 266 he says the Mexicans did not come from the east
through Iceland, Greenland and New France, as Hugo wished; but
from the west and Coro through California and New Mexico.* He
mentions the name in two other places.

---

*Georgi Horni de Originibus Americanis, Libri Qvatvor. Hagae Comitis. Sumptibus
Adriani Vlacq. (1652).
Another edition. Hemipoli. Sumptibus Joannis Mulleri Bibl. 1669. Of these two editions, one
has 283 pages, and the second 503 pages. Both have same date of dedication, 1652. San Francisco Free Public Library. [Destroyed in the fire of 1906].

Father Baegert, S. J., spent sixteen years in Lower California, 1751–1767, was a man of philological tastes, a thorough linguist and made a study of the language of the Waicuri dialect. He is certain the name is not of Indian origin. He cites the explanation of the calida fornax, but does not vouch for its correctnes, although he acknowledges the healthfulness of the climate.

Rev. Dr. Edward Everett Hale quotes the learned Jesuit D. Giuseppe Compoi who believed the word California was composed of the Spanish word 'cala', a little cove or bay, and the Latin word 'fornix', meaning the vault of a building, [also the vaulted opening from which sallies are made.] He applies this to the bay under Cape San Lucas, where an arch is seen under a rock at the western part, and that this arch is as perfect as if constructed by art. And that Cortés thereupon applied the name California to it. We have seen this arch from the anchorage, and it is shown in the volume published by the Hydrographic Office at Washington in 1880;* it does not agree with the good father's account.

Furthermore, we have no proof whatever, that Cortés ever sailed so far west as Cape San Lucas: he remained in the region northeast of San José del Cabo.

The History of California was written in 1757 by the Mexican Jesuit Father Miguel Venegas and afterward translated into English in 1759, and from the latter translated into French in 1767. He says that "until lately it was very imperfectly known that it [California] had been first considered a peninsula, then an island"; and finally he gives credit to Father Kino [Chino] for proving that it was a peninsula [1698–1702.] He evidently overlooked the examinations of Francisco de Ulloa a hundred and fifty years earlier.

He writes that "the name Islas Carolinas was given to this country "in honor of Carolus II of Spain, [1665–1700], when, by his order, "the conquest of California, then thought to be an island, and the "others adjacent, was undertaken with a force equal to the enter-"prise." He then mentions that this name was used in many maps, and adds:

"The name by which the country is at present known, is that of "California, an appellation given to it at its first discovery. Some "use the name in the plural number, calling it the Californias."

---

*THE WEST COAST OF MEXICO * * * No. 56. See sketch opposite page 46.

He wishes he could give the origin and etymology of the name; but none of the Missionaries have found any trace of such a name being given to the country, or harbor, bay, etc.

He cannot subscribe to the name being derived from the two Latin words, calida-fornax, a hot furnace. None of the Conquistadores used such a mode of naming their conquests. He thinks it was possibly derived from some words spoken by the Indians and misunderstood by the Spaniards, and gives examples of such mistakes. There he leaves the matter.

Captain Burney, in writing of the voyage of Cortés to the peninsula of California, says: "In what manner this country came to be "distinguished by the name *California* is left uncertain. It is not "believed that the name was derived from the natives; as the mis- "sionaries who have since resided among the *Californians*, have not "at any time heard of such being applied to any port, bay, or part "of the country. Some have conjectured that on account of the "heat of the weather, Cortés formed the name *California*, from the "Latin words *calida* and *fornax*. But we are not told that there "was greater heat of weather in the peninsula, than on the opposite "coast of *New Spain*; and it has been remarked, that no other of the "names given by Cortés, were immediately from the Latin lan- "guage."*

Then he refers to Bernal Diaz, whom we quote elsewhere.

Captain Beechey, on his visit to the Mission of San Juan, November 1826, recounts his conversations with Father Arroyo, and gives the good padre's explanation of the etymology of the name of the Peninsula of California.† "I shall observe first, [says Beechey] "that it was never known why Cortés gave to the bay which he first "discovered, a name which appears to be composed of two Latin "words *calida* and *fornax*, signifying *heat* and *furnace*, and which "was afterwards transferred to the peninsula." He then refers to Venegas and to Burney whom we have just quoted. He continues: "It was thought in Monterey to have arisen in consequence of a "custom which prevails throughout California, of the Indians shut- "ting themselves in ovens until they perspire profusely, as I have

---

*A Chronological History of the Discoveries in the South Sea or Pacific Ocean, * * * by James Burney, Captain in the Royal Navy. 1803. Four volumes. Quarto. Vol. I. page 178.

†Narrative of a Voyage to the Pacific and Behring's Strait. * * * by Captain F. W. Beechey R. N. *** in the years 1825, 26, 27, 28. London, 1831. Vol. II, page 55.

"already described in speaking of the Temeschal. It is not im-
"probable that the practice appeared so singular to Cortés that he
"applied the name of California to the country, as being one in
"which hot ovens were used for such singular purposes. Padre Ar-
"royo, however, maintained that it was a corruption of *colofon*, which,
"in the Spanish language, signifies resin, in consequence of the pine
"trees which yield that material being so numerous. The first set-
"tlers, he said, at the sight of these trees would naturally exclaim,
"Colofon, which by its similarity to Californo, (in the Catalonian
"dialect, hot oven), a more familiar expression, would soon become
"changed."

In 1878, Professor Jules Marcou made a report to the Chief of
Engineers, Corps of Engineers, U. S. A., entitled "Notes upon the
First Discoveries of California, and the Origin of its Name." Later
he published it in pamphlet form.*

In this report he writes: "Cortés and his companions, struck with
"the difference between the dry and burning heat they experienced,
"compared with the moist and much less oppressive heat of the
"Mexican *tierra caliente*, first gave to a bay, and afterwards ex-
"tended to the entire country, the name of *tierra California*, de-
"rived from *calida fornax*, which signifies fiery furnace, or hot as an
"oven. * * * The author who first employed the name of California
"was Bernardo Diaz of Castillo, who says that Cortés gave the name."

H. H. Bancroft in his History of California† says that the Californians of 1846, Vallejo, and Alvarado agree that the name came
from the words kali forno, upon authority from Baja California; and
meant either a "high hill" or "native land." It looks very much
like the Kal-i-forno, to be mentioned.

He furthermore adds that E. D. Guilbert of Copala, Sinaloa, in-
formed him in 1878 that an old Indian of his locality called the peninsula Tchalifalñi-al, "the sandy land beyond the water." Thos. E.
Slevin, L.L.D., (one of the Councillors of the Geographical Society of
the Pacific), has suggested this was not an Indian word, but the Indian pronunciation of the Spanish word California. This is a highly
probable explanation.

In his History of California, Theo. H. Hittell commences by saying:
"The first account of California that is found in old records, repre-

---

*The first publication was in the ANNUAL REPORT of the Chief of Engineers, U. S. Army,
in 1876. ·

†Volume I. page 66 n, 1885.

"sented it as an island, rich in pearls and gold.   It was said to lie at
"a distance of ten days' journey from the Province of Ciguatan, and
"to be inhabited by women only.* * *   Such was the strange
"story brought to Mexico from Colima by Gonzalo de Sandoval,
"and transmitted by Cortés to the Emperor Charles V., in the latter
"part of the year 1524." He adds in a footnote: "The account is
"contained in the Carta Quarta de Relacion, dated October 15,
"1524."*

Later he refers to the hypotheses of "caliente" and "fornalla";
and the sweat-houses of the Indians. He quotes from Bernal Diaz,
and especially refers to the expression "y entonces toparon con la
California, que es una baia," and suggests that the word 'baia' is a
misprint for 'isla'; but is satisfied that Cortés intended it to cover the
entire country.   Page 53.

A late writer,"M. L." of Fresno, who appears to be well posted on
the subject, and who has evidently examined the geology of Lower
California, expresses the opinion that the name came from the
Indians. In approaching Loreto (on the eastern coast of the peninsula in latitude 26° 10') he saw snow white heaps upon a knoll, and
asked the guide "Que cosa es?"   "Cal y forno" answered the Indian; when he knew at once he had the true meaning and origin of
the name California, because these white heaps were lime kilns; 'cal'
meaning lime, and 'forno' an oven or kiln. He believed that Ulloa,
remembering Montalvo's California, accepted the name for the
country.†

We find no proof that the Indians of Lower California built houses
of stone and mortar, although Diaz says the great edifices of the City
of Montezuma were constructed of cal y canto, stone and mortar.

A recent writer in the "Booklover", 1903, says the true meaning
of the word California has never, to his knowledge, been made
public in America, although he refers to the "Century Dictionary of
Names" (1901) conjuring an "old yarn" about the Esplandian, etc.
He derives it from the Arabic word Kalifat, a province, which he chang-
es to an Arabic—Español compound Kalifon, a great province. Finally he declares the form became Kalif-ornia. He does not believe any one in the United States has seen the original "Las Sergas."

These specimens of guessing indicate that it is time the origin be
made known, so far as usage in Romances, Documents, Narratives,
and Charts furnish evidence.

*History of California by Theodore H. Hittell, 1897. Vol. I, page 37.
†San Francisco Chronicle, June, 1893; New York Herald, June, 1895.

SOME EARLY CHARTS ON WHICH THE NAME CALIFORNIA IS FOUND.

1541.—There was published in 1770 in Mexico in the "Historia de Nueva España" by Francisco Antonio Lorenzana, between pages 328-329, a map bearing the name of the pilot Domingo del Castillo, as maker, with inscription as follows: "Domingo del Castillo, Piloto me fecit en Mexico año del Nacimiento de N. S. Jesu Christo de M.D.XLI." This history is a reprint of the Cortés letters and the map given embraced the shores and islands of the Sea of Cortés as examined by Ulloa, laying down the lower end of the peninsula and the western coast of lower California as far north as Ulloa had reached in 1539, that is, Cape Engaño north of the Island of Cerros or Cedros, in latitude 29° 56′. At that cape Ulloa was baffled by the strong northwesterly winds and returned to New Spain.

Upon this map the name California is placed at the southern extremity of the peninsula. While we have no proof that this name was upon the original chart and not added by Lorenzana in his editing, it seems highly probable that it was placed there by Castillo. If so, it is the first use of the name California upon a chart as far as my knowledge goes.

1542.—Spanish names had found place on the Map of the World by Alonzo de Santa Cruz that indicated a familiarity with the earlier expeditions of the Viceroy Cortés, and the galleons. Mr. E. W. Dahlgren, in describing the map just mentioned, writes: "On the "west coast of Mexico, we see two remarkable inscriptions, Califor-"nia is called 'the island discovered by Marquis del Valle;' page 26, "[Ia. que descubrio el Marques del Valle; page 47], and the coast "north of this point is called 'the land to which Don Antonio de "Mendoza sent out an exploring expedition', page 26; [tierra que "enbio a descubrir don Antonio de Mendoza, page 47]. Thus we "have the two latest geographical dates which have been given a "place on the map. Hernando Cortés, being appointed 'Marques "del Valle de Oaxaca' in 1529, took formal possession of the Cali-"fornia peninsula on the 3rd of May, 1535, although the news did not "reach Spain until after 1537, when Cortés returned to Acapulco." * * * page 26.

"On Santa Cruz's map there is no distinct coast-line north of Cali-"fornia." * * * page 27.

"Thus on this Map of the World we find no *Terra Australis.*"
" * * * page 27.*

1543.—Herrera has a crude chart of part of the west coast of
Mexico, and northward to "C. de Fortun" in latitude 43°. The pen-
insula is named California; and its southern extremity lies in 20°.†
"Descripcion," page 2.

We date this chart soon after 1543 when the expedition of
Cabrillo and Ferrelo, 1542–43, returned to New Spain. Cabrillo
had died at San Miguel Island, in the Santa Barbara Channel,
January 3rd 1543, and chief pilot Ferrelo took command and made
another attempt to follow the coast beyond Punta de Arena, and
saw the high land of the Cape Mendocino region. He probably
made King Peak, in latitude 40° 00', 4090 feet above the sea and
only ten miles inland. On account of a great storm and the
dangers he encountered in this vicinity he named it el Cabo de
Fortunas. This peak is visible seventy-three miles seaward.‡

1559.—"The Interior of New Spain" after Mercator, 1559.** On
this chart off the southeast point of the peninsula is "Calfornia,
alys punta de vallenas." This map has the name India in the southwest part of New Spain.

1570.—Prof. Jules Marcou, in his "Notes upon the First Discovery
of California", says: "Abraham Ortelius, on his map of 1570, en-
"titled *America sive orbis nova descriptio*, wrote at the point indi-
"cating Cape San Lucas the name *C. Cali, formia.* * * * page 6.

"The same geographer, in the first edition of his atlas, *Thea-*
"*trum Orbis Terrarum*, gives, in a map dated 1570, and entitled *Tar-*
"*tario sive Magni Chami Regni*, California as a peninsula with the
"name C. Califormio." * * * ; page 6.

On the "Theatrum Orbis Terrarum," 1570, of Ortelius the scale is
too small to insert these names. This map is a crude attempt of
the homolographic projection.

*Map of the World, by Alonzo de Santa Cruz, 1542. Explanations by E. W. Dahlgren,
Stockholm 1892, large 8vo, pages 48.

†Descripcion de las Indias Occidentales de Antonio de Herrera Coronista Mayor de Sv
Magd. de las Indias y Sucoronista de Castilla. Al Rey Nro. Señor. Madrid, 1730. See map
at page 2 of the Descripcion. It was evidently from this or a similar chart that Michael Lok,
in 1582 laid down the western coast to C. de Fortun in latitude 43°, and thence swung the coast
to the eastward, with the mountains bordering it.

‡Voyages of Discovery and Exploration on the Northwest Coast of America. By
George Davidson. Washington; 1886: see pages 226, 246 and chart.

**From "The Coronado Expedition, 1540–42," by George Parker Winship in the 14th.
Annual Report of the Bureau of Ethnology of the Smithsonian Institution, 1892-93; Part I.

1582.—*C. Californo.* On the queer map of Michael Lok (the promulgator of the Juan de Fuca fiction), the extremity of the peninsula is named "C. Californo." It was published by Hakluyt in 1582, but may have been drawn earlier because it notes among others, the discoveries, "Anglorum 1580," meaning those of the Cabots, Frobisher and Drake. There is, however, no mention of Drake nor of Nova Albion. The Pacific Coast is made to terminate about latitude 44°, and thence strikes eastward under the "Sierre Neuada," to a narrow isthmus in latitude 40°, just north of the "Apal chen" mountains. [Appalachian?]*

1587.—*Punctum Californiae.* In Hakluyt's edition (Paris, 8vo. 1587) of Peter Martyr's *De Orbe Novo* there is a map of the Atlantic and Pacific Oceans, extending from about longitude 10° east to 210° west, through 220°. The Pacific Coast is carried to 50° north and under that parallel is noted "Nova Albion, Inuenta An. 1580, ab Anglis." Cape San Lucas is named "Punctum Californiae." The map as shown is 7¾ inches by 6¾ inches, was presented to Hakluyt by some unknown admirer, and is dated Paris, Cal. Maij, M. D. LXXXVII.

1588–94.—*Californoa.* This is the spelling upon "The Silver Map of the World," which is assumed to be "a contemporary medallion commemorative of Drake's great voyage (1577–80)," * * * by Miller Christy * * * Henry Stevens, Son & Stiles: London, MDCCCC. The diameter of the silver medallion is 2.76 inches; thickness 0.028 inch. Mr. Christy assumes the medallion to have been struck in 1581. We have shown in a paper yet in MS. that the Silver Map must have been engraved after Drake's voyage of 1585–86.

1595.—On the Iodocus Hondius hemispherical map of 1595 (?) he designates the peninsula of Lower California as 'California.' This map contains reports of discoveries to 1588.

1596.—The northern half of De Bry's "America Sive Novus Orbis, 1596," has the peninsula named 'California'. See reference to Coronado's Expedition, by Winship.

---

*The title in Mr. Christy's reduced copy is "Illvstro Viro. Domino Phillipo Sidnæo. Michael Lok Civis Londinensis Hanc Chartam Dedicabat: 1582."

1597.—"Wytfliet's New Granada and California, 1597," in the Coronado Expedition. The title of the map is 'Granata nova et California'; and at the end of the peninsula is 'C. de California,' and between it and the main coast 'Californiæ Sinus', the Gulf of California.

1602-3.—On the chart of the reconnaissance of the northwest coast by Sebastian Vizcaino, drawn up from his thirty-two sub-charts by the officers of the *Sutil y Mexicana* in 1792-1802, the name "Californias" stretches through parts of Upper and Lower California.

1618-1627.—The Hondius Map of the World [Iodocus; Henricus] is quite large; each hemisphere is four feet in diameter. On the peninsula is the name California; at the extremity is C. de California. The title of this map is "Novissima ac Exactissima Totius Orbis Terrarum Descriptio Magna", etc., Amsterdam, 1618; but it took Hondius, Junior, nine years to finish it. He does not use any of Vizcaino's names. The copy we have consulted belongs to Captain Gustave Niebaum of San Francisco. [Destroyed in the Conflagration of April 18-20, 1906.]

1630-1646.—We have photographs of a series of large charts from the Imperial Museum at München which must antedate Dudley's Arcano del Mare of 1630, '46, '47. On one is the "Callifornia R."[egnum], and the "G. della Callifornia"; on another "P. della Callifornia" on the north side of the "R. botta Callifornia," with an anchor to denote an anchorage; latitude 24 1/2°; and "C. di Callifornia" east of San José del Cabo.

On another of these charts there is the legend "Il Regm della Callifornia," but the first three words are crossed out. In latitude 27 degrees is noted "La Costa della Callifornia." In several others are noted "Callifornia," "Callifornia R."[egnum], "C. di Callifornia," "Capo di S. Lucca della Callifornia."

On one chart the cape on the main land directly east of the southern end of the peninsula is denoted "C. dirimpetto la Callifornia"; i. e. Cape opposite to California.

1630-1647.—On Dudley's "Carta prima Generale d'America **" off the southern extremity of the peninsula is "Ia California"; already California had been considered an island.

1647.—In the "Argonauticon Americanorum sive Historiæ periculorum Petri de Victoria ac sociorum eius" by Ioannes Bisselius e Societate Jesu, Libri XV; M. DC. XLVII, there is a chart only 4¾ x 2¾ inches, with the name California on the peninsula, at the head of which is the "Tolmu Regnu." [Tolmum Regnum.]

1671.—On the chart of Arnoldus Montanus, published in Holland, California is laid down as an island that terminates at Cape Blanco north of Cape Mendocino. Along the length of this island is the name "California." An English edition of the book and chart was published in 1672.

1699.—*California I.* In the volumes of Dampier's account of his semi-piratical voyages, 4th Edition, 1699, there are two maps; upon one the name as here given, is applied to the lower part of California, the northern part not being drawn. Upon the western hemisphere "California" is laid down as an island extending to latitude 44°.

1698-1702.—The "Tabula Californiæ Anno 1702" was made from the personal observations of R. Father Eusebius Francisco Chino, S. J. In this he names the gulf and the peninsula "California," and states that he made his journey through the peninsula from latitude 25° to latitude 33°.

It is not necessary to follow the charts of the eighteenth century, yet we mention the "Tabula Californiæ Anno 1702. Ex autoptica observatione delineata à R. P. Chino è S. J." It is devoted to the locations of the missions south of the River Gila and on the eastern coast of the peninsula of California, his "Californiæ Pars." The gulf is named "Mare Californiæ;" and the Pacific is the "Mare del Zur."

We add with some detail a description of a map which we have not seen elsewhere mentioned.

In his "Geographia ó Moderna Descripcion del Mundo," Don Sebastian Fernandez de Medrano*, has introduced a map of America wherein we find some peculiarities of geography and the name California appears twice. The map is seven by six inches and is inserted between pages 220 and 221. It is on a spherical projection

---

*Geographia ó Moderna Descripcion del Mundo, y sus partes, dividida en dos tomos, y compuesta por Don Sebastian Fernandez de Medrano General de Batalla, y Director de la Academia Real y Militar del Exercito de los Payses Baxos. Enriquezida de Cartas Geographicas y mas Estampas. Tomo Primero Amberes. Por Henrico y Cornelio Verdussen. Mercaderes de Libros Año 1709. Size 6⅝ x 4½ inches. 2 Vols. in one. 274 and 296 pages with Indices and plates.

and the central meridian reaches to latitude 75° north and 55° south. On the western coast of North America, "California" is laid down as an island lying in a northwest and southeast direction, and stretching from latitude 22° north to 43° or 44° at the "Fretum Aniani". There is no name given to the long strait or gulf lying between the island and the main land; but the ocean to the westward of the island is the "Mare Californiæ." Of the names of land features we find on the irregular line westward from the Fretum Aniani for twenty degrees of longitude in the latitude of 45° the "Terra Esonis" (Land of Eso or Yezo, Japan?).

The northwestern cape is "C. Blanco" in latitude 41°; "P. d. Monti Ry" in latitude 38°; "Canale d. S. Barbara" in latitude 35°, but the channel and islands are located south of that name.

Point Conception, not named, is in latitude 34°.

We find the "I. d. S. Catalina" in latitude 32½°.

The island of "S. Clement" is fixed to the east of Catalina.   Farther south lies the "I. d. Pararos;" the "P. d. S. Apolline", and "C. Lucas" in its proper latitude.

These are all the names on the chart that relate to California and the northwest coast; but we may state that the "Fretum Aniani" leads eastward into a great sea that approaches the north eastern coast of America.

In the Pacific, south of 20°, he gives the broad ocean the name "Mar del Zur" to latitude 15° S.; "Mare del Zur" along the Mexican and Central American coast; and "Mare Pacificum" south of the tropic of Capricorn.

In the Pacific we find many of the islands of the Hawaiian group with Spanish names, S. Pedro, Los Reis, etc., but they are located ten degrees too far south and too far west.   They recall the group of islands on the Hondius map of 1618-27.

The author has described California in one page of his text, and we give a brief literal translation thereof.

CONCERNING CALIFORNIA.

"Farther to the west [east] and north of the islands of Las Velas [very likely the Ladrones], is that of California (held even to our time to be part of the continent) which has to the eastward the Red Sea [Mar rojo], so named for the same reason as that of Arabia.   To the westward are the limits of the China Sea [Oceano Chinense], which also bathes to the westward the islands of Las Velas and Salomon; to the northward they sweep to the mainland of the Kingdom of Quivira, and to the land to the south is the Mar Pacifico. This comprehends everything between the 23d and 43d degrees of latitude, and between the 237th and 262d degrees of longitude. The traverse from north to south is 350 leagues, from the east to the west is 110 leagues, and the circumference is 1100 leagues. In this area there are many pieces of land uninhabited and sterile, and only at the south are named numerous points and capes which have been discovered and reconnoitred by the Spaniards. All the other islands of the Pacific Ocean and to the south are of little consequence, and so we will pass to those islands which lie to the northward, and to those which are named the Windward and the Leeward Islands."

Then he describes Greenland, Newfoundland, and the West Indies. The whole description of California and the Pacific is erroneous, and not in conformity with the map which he presents. But it will be noted that he gives the southern and northern limits of California as 23° and 43°, agreeing with data to the time of Vizcaino.

The longitudes are reckoned eastward through 360 degrees from the Meridian of Ferro, the southwestern island of the Canaries, in latitude 27°45′ and longitude 17°40′ west from Greenwich.

The leagues given are those of old Spain, and as they are used in other old Spanish narratives we present his explanation of their relation to one degree on the surface of the earth.

THE LENGTH OF AN OLD SPANISH LEAGUE.

Fernandez, in his subdivision "de la Grandeza de la Tierra," pages 40-42, states that the circumference of the terrestrial globe is divided into three hundred and sixty degrees; and that each degree is subdivided into seventeen and one half Spanish leagues; p. 40. And after enumerating the lengths of the subdivision of a degree by Italy, Germany and France, he repeats the former statement and adds that each league contains three and three sevenths miles. This makes the old Spanish league equal to 3.43 geographic miles, or 3.95 English Statute miles.

The author ventures upon stating the circumference of the globe, and its superficial area, and comes remarkably close to modern determinations.

THE FIRST VESSEL NAMED CALIFORNIA.

From 1603 to 1768 Spain was oblivious to the possibilities of California. In 1741 Lord Anson was on the coast of New Spain waiting for the annual treasure ship from the Philippines. He afterwards captured her off the straits of San Bernardino. But Spain continued in her lethargy towards California. The irruption of Captain Cook into the South Sea in 1768-9 awakened her. About this time there was a commercial war in London over the claims of the Hudson's Bay Company as to their rights to territory and the enormous profits of the fur trade, and whether they had discovered the route to the Indies from Hudson's Bay. In this war of rival interests, Mr. Arthur Dobbs formed an opposition company about 1740, and later fitted out two vessels to carry on the fur traffic and if possible open the route to the South Seas.

Part of the exploits of these parties are given in a volume published in London in 1748 containing "An account of a voyage for the discovery of a Northwest passage by Hudson's Streight to the Western and Southern oceans of America, performed in the year 1746 and 1747 in the ship *California*, Captain Francis Smith, commander", by the clerk of the *California*.* The ship is reported as 140 tons.

The use of this name for one of the vessels indicates no doubt that they had in view a voyage along the northwest coast and as far south as California, and is, as far as we know, the first application of the name California to a vessel.

---

*The author's name was Drage. See Barrow's Arctic Voyages, (1818), p. 287.

EARLY SPANISH MENTION OF THE NAME CALIFORNIA
IN NARRATIVES AND DOCUMENTS.

The first mention of the name California which we have found in print is found in Francisco Preciado's diary of the voyage of discovery of Francisco de Ulloa on both coasts of the Gulf of California, and on the Pacific Coast as far north as latitude 29° 56'. This voyage occupied the latter part of 1539 and the early part of 1540. * The vessels were sailing southeastward, close along the eastern coast of the peninsula (October-November), and the narrator says: "We "found ourselves fifty-four leagues distant from California, a little "more or less, always in the southwest seeing, in the night time, "three or four fires." This narrator uses the name California but once; Hakluyt interpolates the "point of California."

Bernal Diaz is the authority most frequently quoted in reference to the naming of the peninsula. In chapter *CC* of his "Historia Verdadera de la Conquista de la Nueva España,"‡ he mentions the name and the circumstances of its application by Cortés. In an appendix we give a few words of his career and standing.

That chapter recounts the supreme efforts which Cortés essayed for the discovery of new lands and new islands. His captains failed him, his ships were lost, and finally he fitted out a last armada and took command himself. He "determined to fulfill his contract "with the Most Serene Empress Doña Isabel, of glorious memory." But failure followed failure. He carried his vessels from Tehuantepec to the westward and northward along the coast to the Gulf of California. After a severe trial, Diaz says, "he was deter- "mined to discover other lands [than Santa Cruz Island, reported "by Ximenes' crew], and by chance came upon California which is "a bay. [Cortés * * * fué à descubrirá otras tierras, y entonces "toparon con la California, que es una bahia.]" He remained at

---

*There is no early Spanish publication or record of his discoveries. The Italian account is in the third volume of the Navigations and Voyages of Gio. Battista Ramusio, pages 339–354, published in Venice in 1565. It was published in English by Hakluyt in 1600 in his Voyages, etc., Vol. III, pages 397–424. The Italian title is too long to quote: see Voyages of Discovery and Exploration on the Northwest Coast of America, Davidson, 1886.

†HISTORY OF CALIFORNIA, H. H. Bancroft. Vol. I, 1542 to 1800, page 65 n.

‡Historia verdadera de la Conquista de la Nueva España escrita por el Capitan Bernal Diaz del Castillo uno de sus Conquistadores. Nueva edicion corregida. Paris, 1837. Four volumes, 12 mo. See Vol. IV. Chapter C C.; pages 335-338.
The original history was not completed until the period of Drake's 1577–80 expedition, but the name and the results of the Ulloa and Cabrillo voyages of discovery had been made public.

this anchorage a long while; then went to New Spain, leaving a
colony at the place.   His vessels returned and carried back to Natividad all the soldiers and captains; [todos los soldados y capi-
tanes que habia dexado en aquella isla ó bahia, que llaman la Cali-
fornia].   Cortés then ordered Captain Francisco de Ulloa to sail
from Natividad on June 15th, 1535, to explore the eastern coast of
the peninsula and lay it down more thoroughly [que corriesen la
costa adelante, y acabasan de baxar la California].   From this account, which Diaz must have received from those who were in the
expedition, it appears that the name was given to a bay or anchorage, to the island protecting that anchorage, and lastly to the
Peninsula.

Herrera mentions the name twice:* "i á los diez de Noviembre,
"continuando siempre la hermosura de la Tierra, se hallaron á cin-
"cuenta i quatro Leguas de la California, pareciendoles siempre, que
"aquella tierra era mui poblada, i toda esta Costa es mui profun-
"da"***Cap. IX, p. 202, col. 1. And about December 15th 1539 Ulloa
discovered the Bay of San Abad, (now Santa Marina Bay in latitude
24° 20′), the southern entrance to Magdalena Bay, where he had
trouble with the Indians and one was killed.   He says the Indians
could not understand the interpreter "que los Castellanos llevaban,
"natural de la Isla de California."   Cap. X, p. 203, col. 2.

Herrera charges Preciado with advising Ulloa to kill the Indians,
and in the Index we find the following statements: "*Francisco
Preciado* aconseja a *Ulloa* embista a los *Indios*, i por que? * * *
pide licencia a *Ulloa* en la *Isla de los Cedros* para matar vn Indio, i se
la niega."

During 1535-37 Ulloa reconnoitered the eastern coast of the
peninsula of California to the Colorado and thence southward, there-
by establishing the geographic relations of the peninsula and continental coasts.

In 1539, with the vessels *Santa Agueda* and *Trinidad* he was ordered to reconnoiter the southern extent of the peninsula, and then
continue northward along the Pacific coast.

*Historia General de los Hechos de los Castellanos * * *   Decada VI, Lib. I, Cap:
VIII, IX, X.

After his failure to beat his sluggish ships more than sixty miles north of Cerros Island against our usual northwest winds and an adverse current, the further exploration of the coast along the Pacific was assigned, in 1542, to Juan Rodriguez Cabrillo, a Portuguese navigator in the service of Spain, and Bartolomé Ferrelo, chief pilot, who were more successful and saw land as far north as King Peak between Point Arena and Cape Mendocino. They did heroic work, and Cabrillo lost his life at San Miguel Island in the Santa Barbara Channel.*

We quote extracts of their reports as given by Herrera:† "Sunday, on the second day of July [1542], they found themselves in "twenty and four degrees and more, and recognized the Port of "Marqués del Valle [Cortés] which is called La Cruz, [Santa Cruz], "which is on the Coast of California;" and the marginal note is to the same effect. Cabrillo.

Ferrelo says: "Sunday, the second day of July [1542], they were "delayed in crossing over [the Gulf of California] by the weather, "which was not favorable, almost four days; they anchored the fol- "lowing Monday, on the third of the same, off the Point of Califor- "nia, and were here two days, and from this place they reached the "Port of San Lucas the following Thursday." In latitude 27° 07', he "says, "were groves of trees which they had not seen from the "Point of California."

In his "Description" Herrera says that "California is a great "point of land that stretches into the sea through several degrees of "latitude; and from its [southern] extremity it reaches towards the "northwest about two hundred leagues; nevertheless it has not re- "ceived much attention, neither its Ports nor Islands in the Gulf of "California" * * *.

The marginal reference is "California"; page 24, column 1.

In his index, Volume VIII, Herrera says that Cortés gave the name; "pusola el nombre California." In the text, Vol. VIII, page 139, column 2, in speaking of Galicia, Culiacan, etc., he writes: "i mas adelante, la California, adonde llegó el primer Marqués del "Valle, que le puso este nombre."

*Voyages of Discovery and Exploration on the Northwest Coast of America, 1539 to 1603. Davidson, 1886.

†HISTORIA, etc. Decada VII, Libro V, Cap. III, p. 89.

After the time of Cabrillo and Ferrelo the galleons of Mexico made their voyages to the Philippines by a nearly direct route with favorable winds; but on their return trip they held well to the northward to catch the northwest winds, and reached the Pacific Coast of America in the latitude of Cape Mendocino, and even higher. We have this clearly stated by the Viceroy, Marqués de Villa Manrique, who wrote to the King of Spain on the 10th of May, 1585:*

"The coast of New Spain ascends from the south even to 42° of "latitude, because your Majesty's ships coming from the Philip- "pines make the land in that latitude, and thence follow the coast to "Gapulco [Acapulco]." A few lines later he speaks of the voyage made to the "Californias" by Cortés. So the name was a matter of common usage. Hakluyt uses it in 1587 in a letter in his Voyages; Vol. III, page 303; published in 1600.

---

*Publications of the Historical Society of Southern California, 1891, page 14. Los Angeles

THE FIRST MENTION OF THE ORIGIN OF THE NAME CALIFORNIA, IN RECENT YEARS.

The first mention we find of the origin of the name California in recent years is made incidentally by George Ticknor in his "History of Spanish Literature." He is comparing the style and meagreness of Esplandian with the eloquence and spirit of Amadis, and writes: "All reference to real history and real geography was apparently "thought inappropriate, as may be inferred from the circumstances, "that a certain Calafria [Calafia], queen of the island of California, "is made a formidable enemy of Christendom through a large part "of the story; and that Constantinople is said at one time to have "been besieged by three millions of heathen. Nor is the style better "than the story. The eloquence which is found in many passages "of the Amadis is not found at all in Esplandian; on the contrary, "large portions of it are written in a low and meagre style," etc. He first published his history in 1849, we quote from the fourth American edition, 1872, Vol. I, page 244.

The second writer who referred to the name California in Las Sergas de Esplandian was Rev. Edward Everett Hale, D. D., who presented a paper on the subject to the American Antiquarian Society, at the Hall of the American Academy in Boston, April 30th, 1862. It was printed the same year.

He introduces the subject by saying that his "attention was acci-"dentally directed a few weeks since to what I think will prove the "origin of the name of California, as applied to the peninsula so "known."

Near the close he says "the original work is now so rare, that I "think the copies in the valuable library of Mr. Ticknor are the only "ones in Massachusetts. To his invaluable collection, and to that "kind courtesy which opens it to every student, and illustrates it "from the treasures of his own studies, am I indebted for all the au-"thorities of value which I am able to cite here."

He refers briefly to Venegas, Diaz and Herrera. Further, to Father Compoi, Clavigero, Rev. Dean French, Powers' Statue of California, Greenhow; and reaches Las Sergas de Esplandian; gives a short quotation naming the Queen and the Island; and notes some of the earlier editions of the romance, and of the later Spanish efforts to introduce it to modern Europeans in 1857. This was done more particularly to illustrate the formation of the language to the present time.   Before this edition D'Herbelay, the early French paraphraser, retained the whole story, but shifted the locality [but not the queen] to the river Borysthenes* and the Riphan mountains; and in 1779, the Count de Tressan published a translation which the reverend writer criticizes somewhat severely, and is in error when he says that the name California is left out in that transfer; see page 563, Vol. II, of the translation.

Dr. Hale concludes by saying that "I know I furnish no etymol-"ogy for that word California," but suggests "the root Calif, as the "Spanish spelling for the sovereign of the Mussulman power of the "time, was in the mind of the author as he invented these Amazon "allies to the Infidel power."

---

*Borysthenes Flu., later Danapris, now Dnieper, which falls into the northern part of the Black Sea about one hundred miles east of Odessa.

THE CAUSES WHICH GAVE RISE TO THE ROMANCES.

In the earlier centuries of the Christian era, from the inexorable code of the duel among the stronger, arose the principles of chivalry. The leaders throughout Christendom held its demands sacred beyond all other considerations. It was the religion of might, and of right as they understood this.

When Peter the Hermit aroused Europe in the eleventh century to recover the Holy Sepulchre from the Turks, the opportunity for the development of chivalry for a high purpose was presented, and tens of thousands enlisted or were forced under the Banner of the Cross. History has no parallel to the madness that lasted through two centuries. From this fanaticism and frenzy was evolved a reckless spirit of adventure and of enterprise.

The religious-military orders of Templars, Knights-Hospitallers of St. John of Jerusalem, and others, were founded for the delivery of the Holy Land from the Turks, and naturally there arose many religious and military orders or organizations which are represented today.

From the exploits of the Crusaders, the knights and kings, real or unreal, there necessarily grew the wonderful, unnatural and impossible Romances, of which the Round Table of King Arthur, and the Paladins of Charlemagne are well known examples.

Traditions were conjured, Amazons created, giants, griffins and unknown beasts of land, air and water were brought forth for every emergency. The Terrestrial Paradise was the region to be discovered in the far east.

In one generation Spain closed the centuries of warfare against the Moors; she expelled a hundred thousand of her Jewish population. With peace reigning and industry nearly destroyed, her young nobles sought new fields for enterprise. The daring sea explorations of the Portuguese aroused Spain to the opening of a vast, unknown field for exploitation. Columbus appeared, and Isabella saw the discovery of a new world. Then quickly followed the conquest of Mexico, of Central America, of Peru, and the countries of the Amazon and the Orinoco.

The ardent soul of Spain was awakened. In fifty years her fleets had passed the Strait of Magallanes, crossed the Pacific, and discovered the Philippines. She circumnavigated the globe; her traffic crossed the Pacific to the occident; and her discoverers reached nearly to Cape Mendocino.

No romance read by her nobles and her people, approached the height of such supreme accomplishments.

It is not to be marvelled that when the Romances began to appear they were seized upon by the people, who had little to read save some dry treatises of philosophy or theology. They were to be found everywhere; edition after edition appeared in different places. The traditions of the days of the Crusades were still recited, and these new Romances seemed the verification of the old stories. They were read, discussed, and were an intellectual enjoyment of the people, high and low.

Their reading was not confined to Spain; the Amadis was translated into French, Italian, Dutch, English, German, and even into Hebrew. Robert Southey translated the Amadis.

Ticknor says that "we have abundant proof that the fanaticism "for these romances was so great in Spain during the sixteenth "century, as to have become matter of alarm to the more judicious.

"Many of the distinguished contemporary authors speak of the "mischiefs, and from different sources we know that many who "read the fictions took them for true histories. The evil, in fact, had "become formidable and the wise began to see it. At last these "romances had been deemed so noxious, that in 1553 they were pro- "hibited by law from being printed or sold in the American colo- "nies, and in 1555 the same prohibition, and even the burning of all "copies of them then extant in Spain itself, was earnestly asked for by "the Cortes. And this prohibition would have become a law were it "not that the abdication of the emperor, the same year, stopped "action upon it."

The passion for this class of literature gradually abated, and at last died out when Cervantes attacked it with exquisite ridicule.

THE HISTORIAN TICKNOR'S ESTIMATE OF THE ROMANCE AMADIS DE GAULA.

He says that in the extraordinary and innumerable family of Romances the Amadís is the poetical head and type. The author "certainly had a knowledge of the old French Romances, such as "that of Saint Graal or Holy Cup:—the crowning fiction of the "Knights of the Round Table."

He then traces the Original to Vasco de Lobeira, a Portuguese gentleman attached to the court of John of Portugal. *** "He "died in 1403. * * * Our first notice of it is from a grave "statesman, Ayala, the Chronicler and the Chancellor of "Castile, who died in 1407 * * * Gomez Eannes de "Zurara, keeper of the archives of Portugal in 1454, * * * leaves "no substantial doubt that the author of the Amadis of Gaul "was Vasco de Lobeira."* As Lobeira died in 1403, that carries the date earlier than 1400. The original has been undiscovered. A manuscript copy existed as late as 1750. It is supposed to have been burned in the palace of the Dukes of Arveiro in 1755.

The Spanish version was made between 1492 and 1504 by Garcia Ordoñes de Montalvo, and very probably was printed before 1504, because Montalvo (page 235 n.) says in his prólogo that both of the Catholic Sovereigns were still alive, and it is known that Isabella died in 1504. Montalvo wrote the Esplandian perhaps before he published the Amadis, and introduced it as the fifth Amadis.

The purpose of the Amadis was to set forth the character of a perfect knight so as to illustrate the virtues of courage and chastity as the only proper foundation of such a character. Page 237. The Amadis is admitted by general consent to be tbe best of all the old romances of chivalry. * * * The Amadis, therefore, was a work of extraordinary popularity in Spain; and one which, during the centuries of its greatest favor, was more read than any other book in the language. Page 241.

To show that its popularity was genuine Mr. Ticknor adduces testimony from Cervantes:

---

*HISTORY OF SPANISH LITERATURE, George Ticknor. 2nd edition, 1854, pages 221, 222, Vol. I.

Even when "the avenging satire of Cervantes" * swept away the
whole of the Romances, we see that he "was not insensible to its
"merits. * * * The first book that, as he tells us, was taken from
"the shelves of Don Quixote, when the curate, the barber, and the
"housekeeper began the expurgation of his library, was the Amadis
"de Gaula. * * * 'There is something mysterious about this
"matter,' quoth the curate; 'for, as I have heard, this was the first
"book of knight-errantry that was printed in Spain, and all the
"others have had their origin and source here, so that, as the arch-
"heretic of so mischievous a sect, I think he should, without a hear-
"ing, be condemned to the fire.' 'No Sir,' said the barber, 'for I,
"too, have heard that it is the best of all the books of its kind that
"have been written, and, therefore, for its singularity, it ought to
"be forgiven.' 'That is the truth', answered the curate, 'and so let
"us spare it for the present"; a decision, which, on the whole, has
been confirmed by posterity, and precisely for the reason Cervantes
has assigned.   Pages 243, 244.

Mr. Ticknor might have continued a little further:

"The next one, said the barber, is the Exploits of Esplandian, the
"son of Amadis de Gaula.   Verily, said the curate, the goodness of
"the father shall not avail the son.   Throw him into the yard and
"let him make a beginning of the pile for the intended bonfire."
And so Esplandian was doomed to the flames. [Translation by
Charles Jarvis.]

---

*"Al immortal Cervántes estaba reservado el aniquilar de un solo golpe los libros de cabal-
lerias."   Don Pascual de Gayangos.   "

BERNAL DIAZ, ONE OF THE CONQUISTADORES, AND HISTORIAN OF THE EXPLOITS OF CORTES, HAD READ THE AMADIS DE GAULA.

At the time when Cortés with his victorious army was approaching the city of Montezuma, Diaz writes: "The discourse with the "Caciques was finished and we immediately moved toward the city. "The chiefs had brought with them so many people from the sur- "rounding districts to see us that the roads were filled with them.

"The next morning we reached the broad highway of Iztapalapa, "which is straight and level as any that exists in Mexico. There we "halted, and thence beheld many cities and towns in the water, "[of the lake], and on the firm land were others with multitudes of "people. We were seized with admiration, and declared they "seemed like the castles of enchantment recorded in the book of "Amadis [de Gaula.] Grand towers, temples and edifices that "seemed to rise from the water. And all these were constructed of "stone and mortar, [cal y canto.] Some of our soldiers said they "could not be sure whether they were really seeing this or were "dreaming.

"And it must not be wondered that I, on the spot, should de- "scribe the scene in this manner, and which I have long pondered. "We have beheld unnumbered things that have never been heard "of, never seen, and never dreamed of." Diaz continues his des- criptions; and devotes Chapter LXXXVIII to "el gran é solemne "recebimiento que nos hizo el gran Montezuma á Cortés, y á todos "nosotros en la entrada de la gran ciudad de México."*

See appendix for Diaz's life.

---

*HISTORIA VERDADERA DE LA CONQUISTA DE LA NUEVA ESPANA, ESCRITA POR EL CAPITAN BER- NAL DEL DIAZ DEL CASTILLO, UNO DE SUS CONQUISTADORES. Nueva edicion corregida. Paris, Li- breria de Rosa. 1837, 4 Vols., duo: see Vol. II, pages 67, 68.

THE MYTHICAL AMAZONS, THE GRIFFINS, AND THE TERRESTRIAL PARADISE.

Ancient medals and monuments represent the Amazons in warlike costume. They used bows and arrows, javelins, an axe of peculiar shape, and bucklers in the form of a half moon. They are said to have founded an empire along the south and east coasts of the Black Sea, with their principal seat on the river Thermodon which empties near the southernmost part of that sea.

Homer relates that when Priam was encamped with the Phrygians on the banks of the Sangarius (Saggários) the Amazons ('Αμαζόνες) equal-to-men joined them.*

Their queen Penthesilea, who invented the battle axe, aided in the defence of Troy.

Herodotus particularly decribes the battle fought between the Greeks and the Amazons on the Thermodon, with their defeat and being carried into captivity.

Diodorus Siculus says there was a nation living on the Thermodon that was governed by women, who managed all military affairs. He also mentions another race of Amazons who dwelt in Africa and that they were of greater antiquity than those on the Thermodon.

Plutarch, in his life of Theseus, treats of the Amazons, and considers the accounts which have been preserved of them as partly fabulous and partly true. In his life of Pompey he locates them in the Caucasus, and on the Thermodon.

Quintus Curtius details the visit of Queen Thalestris of the Amazons to Alexander the Great; it is mentioned by other authorities, and Justin says it required a twenty-five days' march.

This fable of the Amazons survived classical antiquity, and came down through the centuries to the days of chivalry and romance; but we need only refer to the first letter of Columbus to be satisfied that the early navigators brought the fables to the western world, and cultivated them on new soil.

Francisco de Orellana's chronicler, the Dominican Fray Gaspar de Carvajal, transplanted the fable to regions of the Amazon River, in the wild search for "el hombre dorado." In 1522 Cortés sent Gonçalo de Sandoval to succor Christoval de Olid who had gone to Colima. and from him we have the report of a very rich island peopled

---

*ILIAD: Book III, lines 187-8: The mouth is eighty miles east of the Bosporus.

with Amazons, ten days' journey from Colima. This legend appears in the fourth letter of Cortés to the Emperor Carlos V, dated Oct. 15, 1524.* In 1529 a large expedition left Mexico to continue the discoveries of Olid and Sandoval, but especially to reach the island.

In the Historia de Nueva España escrita por su esclarecido Conquistador Hernan Cortés, aumentada con otros documentos, y notas; por el Ilustrisimo Señor Don Francisco Antonio Lorenzana, Arzobispo de Mexico, etc., 1770, this story is given in detail. As a matter of history it eventually killed the legend of the Amazons.

We find a unique illustration of the persistence of the belief in Dourado's chart of the Coasts of Mexico and California, under date of 1580.† In the country east of "La Mar Bermeia," or Vermilion Sea, [Gulf of California], there are three groups of two Amazons in each, armed with bows, and seeking game. The figures are drawn over one inch in height, *in puris naturalibus.* There are also two caballeros on horseback armed with long spears, and one of them is attacking a mazama. In other places are spotted deer.

The belief in the Amazons was not confined to the Conquerors of Mexico; it preceded their advent, and was extended to both the Americas.

Columbus heard of the Amazons on his first voyage. In his letter of March 4, 1493, in speaking of the Caribs, he says:‡

"They are the same who have intercourse with the women on the "first island which is found on the voyage from Spain to the Indies, "on which no men live. These do not follow any womanly occupa- "tions, but use bows and arrows of cane, like those mentioned above, "and cover and arm themselves with brazen plates, of which they "have many. * * *

---

*Venegas repeats the legend and explains it. Vol. I, pages 131–132.

†Our photographic copy of the chart No. 13, from Cod. Iconogr. 137, in the Royal Museum of München is within half a centimeter of the size of the original which is 47 cm. by 64 cm. Mr. Edward W. Mealey. U. S. Consul. wrote to us saying that the original was elaborately drawn on parchment. It is a curious and inaccurate delineation of the coast, but we can locate some of the places on the coast, as "Puerto de Nauidad de aqui Sale llas naues para maluco," in latitude 19½°; "C: Bllanico feza des poblada," in latitude 34° which we believe is Point Concepcion. Beyond this all is vague guess work to Rui Lopez de Villalobos. west of the great strait. in latitude 41°, and 620 leagues west by north from Point Concepcion. Rui Lopez de Villalobos was never on the California Coast.

‡THE GILDED MAN, ELDORADO: Bandelier, page 113.

"The legend of the Amazons was unquestionably domiciled upon
"the American continent by the Spaniards, and was suggested by
"imperfectly understood accounts of distant tribes given by the
"natives, to whose words the Spaniards were not inattentive."

The legend appears first in the fourth letter of Cortés to the Emperor Carlos V, dated October 15, 1524:

"And among the reports which he [Gonzalo Sandoval] brought
" from that province [Colima] was an account of a very good harbor
"(puerto escondido), [Acapulco ?—D.] which was found on that coast;
" * * * and also he told me of the lords of the province of Cigua-
"tan, that many of them asserted there was an island inhabited only
"by women without any grown man among them, and that from
"time to time men went out to them from the mainland; *** when
"they bore daughters they kept them, but the sons were put away.
"This island is ten days' distance from the province and many of the
"principal men had gone there from the province and had seen them.
"I was also told they were rich in pearls and gold."   Page 114.

"On the 20th December, 1529, Nuño Beltrán de Guzman, at the
"head of a large Spanish squadron and more than eight thousand
"Indians left [the city of] Mexico for the purpose of continuing the
"discoveries begun by Sandoval for Cortés in the northwest. * * *
"His march was directed first toward Miochoacan, but its ultimate
"goal was the gold-rich and pearl-bearing island of the fabulous
"Amazons."   Page 119.

"This expedition was a bitter disappointment. Sandoval had
"brought the story of the Amazons from Cihuatlan in the present
"state of Sinaloa; but instead of the island on which he had placed
"the soldierly women, Guzman was shown only a few insignificant
"villages. He found them, however, exclusively inhabited by
"women and children, for the men had fled to the mountains. The
"legend of the Amazons was thus resolved into those mistakes sure
"to arise at that time on the first contact of Europeans with natives
"whose language they could not understand. No trace was found
"of gold, pearls, or treasures of any kind. The story of the Ama-
"zons ceases from this time to be of any significance in the history
"of discovery in the northern half of America."   Page 122.

It may be added that the habitat of the Amazons extended to
South America, in fact over nearly the whole region where the early
Spanish adventurers and discoverers forced their way. In the
northern regions of South America there was a wonderful amount

of energy wasted in the search for 'el hombre Dorado,' or the gilded
man; and we quote, from page 64:

"The fable of the Amazons survived from classical antiquity as
"one of the cycle of myths that were credited or held possible.   In
"Francisco de Orellana's chronicles, the Dominican Fray Gaspar de
"Carvajal transplanted it to the banks of the great South American
"River. * * * This arose from a simple statement that below the
"mouth of the Rio Negro women took part in the fighting against
"the Spaniards.   Another statement was an account by a captive
"Indian of a tribe of Amazons, rich in gold, living north of the river.
"*** The Amazon River henceforward formed the southern bound-
"ary of the mythical region within which 'el hombre Dorado' could
"still find a place."   Page 64.

THE GRIFFINS OF THE ROMANCES.

The Griffin is seen on ancient medals, and the chariot of the Sun
was drawn by these imaginary animals with the head and wings of
the Eagle and the body and legs of the Lion.   They represented
strength and activity.   Having been adopted by the Greeks and
the Romans in ornamental architecture they became a common
representation of the marvellous to writers of the Romances.   And
the belief in their existence comes down to a very late day.

The Griffins of Queen Calafia play a very picturesque but un-
fortunate part in her assault upon the walls of Constantinople.

Bisselius (1647) says of the western coast of North America:
"Chains of mountains stretch along the coast horrifying by their
"sharpness and steepness to their very peaks.   Wonderful numbers
"of wild animals abound among their fastnesses.   People tell that
"in the forests the *Gryphes* [Griffins] are found; and this is not a fable
"but the truth. *** Along this coast is located the land of *Cali-
"fornia.*"

THE TERRESTRIAL PARADISE.

The earlier peoples of Europe discussed the location of the Garden of Eden. Among other surmises it was imagined to be upon a high mountain area overlooking the greater part or all of the earth, and that from it flowed the four large rivers of the world, the Ganges, the Tigris and Euphrates, and the Nile.

Sir John Mandeville who went to the east in 1322 says, [Warren, page 7,] "And beyond the land and isles and deserts of Prester John's "lordship *** there is the dark region *** which lasts from this coast "unto terrestrial paradise, where Adam our first father, and Eve "were put."

The wise men say, "that the terrestrial paradise is the highest "place of the earth, and it is so high that it nearly touches the circle "of the moon as she makes her turn." But the shrewd narrator closes: "of paradise I cannot speak properly, for I was not there."

In 1798, Columbus on his third voyage discovered the island he named Trinidad, off the delta of the river Orinoco, in latitude $10\frac{1}{2}°$ north. He sailed around it through the Gulf of Cuparipari (Paria) and through the Dragon's Mouth having the island and the mainland in view; he continued west along the continental shore, Venezuela, as far as Margarita Island. He believed that he had discovered so great a protuberance of the earth's surface that he believed our globe pear-shaped; and in his letter to the King quoted scripture about the earthly paradise, the area in which the four great rivers had their source. He could find no Roman or Greek authority for its location; nor had he seen it on any map; but he had learned that all the learned theologians had fixed it in the east. He is satisfied that the "earthly paradise" is near the equinoctial line, that it can never be reached except by special providence. The blandness of the climate, the immense volume of fresh water coming from many large rivers, the opinions of holy and wise theologians, conspire to satisfy him that "the terrestrial paradise is situated at the spot I have described." Columbus evidently believed he had reached the land of India where the Garden of Eden had been indefinitely located.

THE ORIGIN AND MEANING OF THE NAMES CALIFORNIA AND CALAFIA, AND ASSOCIATED NAMES, IN LAS SERGAS DE ESPLANDIAN AND AMADIS DE GAULA.

A condensation of the title of Las Sergas is: "El Ramo que de "los quatro Libros de Amadis de Gaula sale; llamado Las Sergas del "Muy Esforzado Caballero Esplandian, hijo del Excelente Rey "Amadis de Gaula."* And the edition of 1510 was generally attributed to Garcia Ordoñez de Montalvo.

The expanded explanation of the title announces that it was written in Greek by the "Gran Maestro Elisabat, who saw and took "part in what he relates."

To keep up the illusion of this romance having been written in Greek there are several proper names of persons and places introduced in this, and in the earlier romance "Amadís de Gaula." The base word of these names is the Greek κάλλος (kállos), meaning beauty.

The Greek dictionary states that the form καλλι- (kalli) in compound words gives the idea of beautiful to the simple word, or is like a mere adjective with its substantive. Numerous examples are given as καλλίκερως (kalli-keros), with beautiful horns; καλλίνικος (kalli-nikos), with glorious victory; καλλιόπη (kalli-ope), the beautiful-voiced; καλλίφυλλος (kalli-phyllos), with beautiful leaves, etc.

The grand master Elisabat was simply following the highest authority, where we find Paris ending his address to Hector: "May "you inhabit the very fertile Troy; but let the Greeks return to "horse-feeding (ἱππόβοτον) Argos and Achæa abounding-in- "beautiful-women (καλλιγύναικα)."†

With this short exhibit we propose the following explanation for the construction of the names which Elisabat has given to his heroine, her island, and to other persons and places.

---

*The Exploits of the very Powerful Caballero Esplandian, Son of the Admirable King Amadis of Gaul.
 The title of the volume containing the Amadis and Esplandian is: BIBLIOTECA DE AUTORES ESPANOLES desde la formacion del lenguaje hasta nuestros dias. Libros de Caballerias, con un discurso preliminar y un catálogo razonado por Don Pascual de Gayangos, individuo de la Real Academia de la Historia. (Coat of Arms.) Madrid, M. Rivadeneyra, editor. * * * 1880 Administracion: Madera Baja, Num. 8, 1880. The sixth edition of the modern publication of January, 1857. We use that of 1880, 580 large octavo pages, double columns. The Public Library of Boston has a copy of the edition published at Burgos in 1587; and we have negative photograph plates of the title and first page.

†The Iliad, Book III, line 74.

I. CALAFIA; "The Queen of the island of California;" from καλλι-, beautiful, and φίλη, (phile) a female friend; or more probably from καλλιφυής (kalliphues), of beautiful and noble stature. "La muy esforzada reina Calafia, señora de la gran isla "California, donde engrande de abundancia el oro y las preciosas "piedras de crian." "Of beautiful growth and shape was the Queen of "California who gave such unexpected and marvellous succor to the "Turks against the Christians, who were defending Constantinople. " * * * She was of majestic proportions; more beautiful than all "other women, and in the full flush and vigor of her womanhood."

The name Calafia is introduced seventeen times.

II. CALIFORNIA; from κάλλος, beauty, or καλλι-, beautiful, and ὄρνις (ornis), a bird. "In this island are many griffins * * * which can be found in no other part of the world." The queen took five hundred of these griffins to assist in the capture of Constantinople.

The name of this island is introduced ten times and is vaguely described and located, as we shall show by quotations.

The double λ of the Greek has a value different from the double l of the Spanish and is best represented by a single l, although some of the München manuscript charts have a double l. The letter f is introduced by epenthesis for the sake of euphony.

III. CALAFERA; the name of an island, the lord of which was Garlante. From καλλι-, beautiful, and φέρω, (phero), to bear along with the sense of motion; or more likely, φήρ, plural φῆρες (pheres), the Centaurs. This name is used but once. A further account of this island is given later.

IV. CALIFAN," a beautiful villa or town belonging to Barsinan, lord of San Sueña." From καλλι-, beautiful, and φανός [phanos], bright, etc.

This name is used twice in the Amadis de Gaula.

V. CALIFENO EL SOBERBIO, Califeno the Superb; one of the forty bravest Caballeros. From καλλι-, beautiful, and φένω (pheno), to slay. Sobérbio, the superb, proud, haughty, arrogant.

The name and designation are used once.

Later on we have suggested that the name of Calafia's sister, Liota, who defended her with lion-like fierceness, was derived from the Greek.

TRANSLATIONS FROM LAS SERGAS CONCERNING THE ISLAND OF CALIFORNIA AND CALAFIA, THE QUEEN THEREOF.

GARLANTE, THE LORD OF CALAFERA.

"Concerning Esplandian and the other Caballeros who went in "the ship of la Gran Serpiente, who had great desire to visit Urgan- "da la Desconocida, who, since having spoken about many things "at the village of Galacia, sailed with them. * * *

"Let us go, said Urlanda, to the village and leave in this small "vessel my maidens and my dwarfs, and send at once for Norandel. "There is no reason why this voyage should be made without so "good a Caballero; and I will bring to you your best friend the King "of Dacia whom I found wounded after a combat which he had with "Garlante, the Lord of the Island Calafera, because he sought to "seize two maidens whom he had with him in his ship. Then the "king as a good Caballero, fought with him, and notwithstanding "the great risk to his life, he finally overcame him and was prepared "to decapitate him, when he pleaded for mercy and begged to "have his life spared. The king pardoned him, and made him "swear that he would never use the knighthood in any other man- "ner than what he commanded."*

QUEEN CALAFIA AT THE DEFENCE OF CONSTANTINOPLE.

"Concerning the spontaneous and unexpected succor which "the Queen Calafia rendered in favor of the Turks at the harbor of "Constantinople.

"I wish that you should now know of a matter so very strange, "that neither in writings nor from the memory of people, is it pos- "sible to discover how on the following day the city was on the point "of being lost, and how in that moment of peril it was saved.

"Know ye that at the right hand of the Indies there is an island "named California, very close to that part of the Terrestrial Para- "dise, which was inhabited by black women, without a single man "among them, and that they lived in the manner of Amazons. They "were robust of body, with strong and passionate hearts and great "virtues. The island itself is one of the wildest in the world on ac- "count of the bold and craggy rocks. Their weapons were all made

---

*Chapter CVIII. pages 508-509.

"of gold; and also the trappings of their wild animals with which they
"make their forays after being domesticated. * * *

"The island everywhere abounds with gold and precious stones:
"and upon it no other metal was found. They lived in caves well
"excavated. They had many ships with which they sailed to other
"coasts to make forays; and the men whom they took as prisoners
"they killed in the manner to be hereafter described. * * *

"In this island, named California, there are many griffins on ac-
"count of the great ruggedness of the country which was infested
"with wild animals. In no other part of the world can they be
"found. * * *

"Whenever a man came to the island he was promptly killed and
"eaten. * * *

"From the time when those grand men of the Pagans departed
"with their great fleets, as recorded in history, there ruled over that
"island of California a queen of majestic proportions, more beautiful
"than all others, and in the very vigor of her womanhood. She was
"desirous of accomplishing great deeds; she was valiant and cour-
"ageous, and ardent with a brave heart, and had ambitions to exe-
"cute nobler actions than had been performed by any other ruler.

"She listened to what others related how the larger part of the
"world expressed themselves against the Christians, and did not
"understand what Christians were because she obtained her in-
"formation not directly from other countries, but from the reports of
"neighboring islands. Anxious to see the world, and the peoples of
"other islands, and believing that with their great fortitude and hero-
"ism, everything could be safely gained step by step, she addressed
"her women and declared she would give them her full support; and
"that it would be best for them to go in her large ships, following
"that route which the grand princes and the great men had taken.
"She animated and encouraged them by narrating the high honors
"and many advantages that would accrue to them from such a voy-
"age. Above all she pictured the undying fame which the whole
"world would accord to them, and contrasted these glories with the
"quiet life on this island, where they did nothing but what their an-
"cestors did; where they would continue to live in a tomb, like walk-
"ing ghosts, and the present and the future would pass without
"fame or glory, as with brute animals. So many things were in-
"stilled into them by this noble Queen Calafia. that she not only

"moved them to consent to her proposition, but they made imme-
"diate preparation for the voyage because they would so much the
"sooner meet those great personages.

"The Queen with the good disposition which marked her life,
"without more delay, ordered the fleet to be provisioned, everything
"necessary to be put on board, with all the golden arms; and gave
"particular orders to have the largest vessel fitted as a vast cage
"with large wooden gratings wherein to confine five hundred griffins,
"which I have already told you were fed upon the men captured
"in battle; and she carried also the animals which they were to
"ride in the forays; and selected the best women, and those best
"armed, for service in the fleet, leaving on the island only those
"that were necessary for its protection. Her preparations were
"so quickly executed that the fleet put to sea and opportunely ar-
"rived at the rendezvous of the pagan fleet the night of the great
"batte, as I shall relate. Great joy and harmony pervaded the
"fleets, and very soon the Queen's vessels were visited by the great
"personages who complimented her and her companions very highly.

"She was very anxious to learn how the contest stood, and to
"learn all the details up to the time of her arrival. After learning
"which she said: 'You have fought bravely in endeavoring to take
"this city with your large numbers, and although you have failed,
"yet with my forces I wish on the morrow to show you that their
"power will suffice to overcome the enemy, if you will accept my
"advice.' Then all the great commanders begged her to state the
"plans she proposed to effect the conquest. She answered: 'At
"once issue orders to all your captains that to-morrow they shall not
"move, nor shall you leave your camp-quarters until I give the or-
"der: and you shall see a battle, the strangest ever seen and never
"before dreamed of.' This was promptly made known to the Grand
"Sultan of Liguia and to the Sultan of Halapa who had command of
"the army in the field; and by these made known to the troops, who
"all wondered what could cause so great a change through that
"Queen."*

"As the night rolled by and the day broke, the Queen Calafia
"landed from her vessel. She and her Amazons were well armed
"with weapons of gold, all covered with the most precious stones

---

*Chapter CLVII, pages 539-540.

"that are found on the island of California in great abundance.
"And she ordered that one of the doors of the large cages that con-
"tained the griffins should be opened. The animals came forth in a
"wild scramble, and seeing the land around them they flew up in
"the air with apparent delight, and soon they espied many people
"walking about. They were very hungry and being without fear
"they each seized a man, and carrying them to the housetops and
"high places they began to eat them. Many arrows were shot at
"them, and they received heavy blows from the lances and swords,
"but their feathers were so thick and strong that their flesh was
"never hurt. This was the most uncommon but satisfactory hunt-
"ing that had ever been witnessed. When the Turks saw the grif-
"fins carrying their enemies through the air they gave vent to the
"loudest exclamations of rejoicing, that reached the very heavens;
"but it was very sad and most painful to those in the city who were
"unable to bear it, when the father saw carried away the son, the son
"the father, the brother the brother; and their floods of tears, their
"wailings and their furious actions excited the greatest compassion.

"After the griffins had sailed through the air for some time, and
"had dropped their prey, they descended to the ground and to the
"sea at their starting point, and without any sign of fear seized
"many others, at which their people were doubly rejoiced, and the
"Christians cast down in the greatest grief. What shall I say? The
"fear upon those on the walls was so great that had it not been
"possible for some of them to conceal themselves under the arches
"of the towers which afforded protection, (all the others having dis-
"appeared), there would have been no one left to defend them.

"When this was seen by Queen Calafia, she commanded, in a loud
"voice, the officers to order their men to the walls with the scaling
"ladders, and capture the city by assault. Then all rushed for-
"ward with the greatest alacrity, fixed their ladders and scaled the
"walls. The griffins which had already dropped their captives,
"saw the soldiers making the assault, and not knowing friend from
"foe, seized the Turks in the same manner that they had seized the
"Christians, and soaring high in the air with them, let them drop to
"the earth and thus killed every one of them.

"Joy was changed to tribulation. Those on the one side exhib-
"ited the deepest sorrow; and those within the walls seeing their
"enemies seized on the walls experienced much joy. At this time

"those Turks who were on the ramparts were terrified, and expected
"to be destroyed by the griffins as their comrades had been. The
"Christians sallied from the arches, and in a very short time killed
"many of the Turks who were between the walls and the houses, and
"made the others come down, and again retreated to the arches when
"they saw the griffins flying toward them.

"When this was seen by Queen Calafia she was sad in a grand
"manner, and exclaimed: 'My idols, in whom I believe and whom I
"adore, what is this that makes my coming as favorable to my en-
"emies as to my friends? I believe that with your support and
"with the complete preparations which I have made we shall de-
"stroy the enemy: this trouble must stop here.' And then she gave
"orders to her Amazons to bring the scaling ladders, and assault the
"towers; kill all those who should be captured; and secure the grif-
"fins. To obey and execute the command of their Queen they
"quickly dismounted, and placed over their bosoms half the skull of
"a fish, while their bodies were covered so strongly that no weapon
"could pierce them. The armor of their bodies and arms and legs
"was of gold, as I have already described. They marched rapidly
"toward the walls, placed the scaling ladders and mounted with
"great agility. From the walls they commenced the fight with the
"enemy under the protection of the arches. But when attacked at
"close quarters, with the gates so small, the latter defended them-
"selves bravely. But those of the city who were under the pro-
"tection of the walls wounded some of the Amazons, with their
"arrows and lances; and thus the women were attacked on both
"sides, and found their arms of gold were weak. The griffins
"were hovering over head without having been noticed, so that
"when the Queen Calafia saw this, she said to the officers, 'order
"your soldiers to the walls that my soldiers may defend and
"protect my birds from attack.' Very soon the Sultans ordered
"some of their soldiers to scale the walls, and hold them and the
"towers, because by night all the army would support them,
"and the city would be stormed. Coming from their encampment
"at a quick pace they climbed upon the wall where the women could
"fight; and very soon some griffins saw them and became so furious
"that during the day they managed to seize some of the soldiers.
"The women attacked the birds with their knives, caring nothing
"for their wild nature, but the griffins would, at times, seize a sol-

"dier by force, and flying high with their prey let him fall to his
"death.   The fright of the Turks was extremely great, and many
"who were scaling the walls became so terrified that they gave up the
"attempt and retreated to the encampment.   The Queen who saw
"them skedaddle (desbarate sin remidio) utterly demoralized, sent
"for the women on the vessel who had charge of the griffins, to call the
"birds off and lock them in their cages. These women, hearing the
"command of the Queen, climbed high on the ship, and in their lan-
"guage with a loud voice called them back.   And, as if they were hu-
"man beings, they all went on board, and obediently went into their
"cages."*

Chapter CLX is quite long and full of the fury of a great battle.
Part of the heading indicates the aggressiveness and activity of the
Queen:

                              *   *   *

                  "Y como Calafia, la espada en la mano,
                  Hace gran daño con sus Amazones,
                  Donde murieron muy muchas personas
                  De fieles, y mas del bando pagano."

The Queen imagined that the Sultans had doubts of the value of
her assistance which she was determined to wipe out.   So at her re-
quest they ordered the army to make a vigorous attack upon the
walls, while her fleet was attacking the city by water.   The attack
upon the walls was repulsed, and those who had scaled them were
thrown down.   When Calafia saw this repulse she rushed with
the   Amazons   upon   the   principal gate   Aquileña   which was
guarded by Norandel, the half brother of Amadis.   She advanced
rapidly before the others, and he came forth to meet her.   Both
met in full career with such force that each lance was broken upon
the other's shield, but neither was unhorsed.   Norandel drew his
sword and Calafia her large knife, (un gran cuchillo), and they fought
so desperately that the Amazons and the Christians came to the support of their chiefs, and a general battle was on.

The narrator Elisabat was there and declares, "that the deeds
"which the Queen did in arms, such as slaying knights and unhors-
"ing them wounded, how she rushed upon her enemies so auda-
"ciously that no one would have believed or dreamed any woman

---

*Chapter CLVIII, pages 240–241.

"abounded with so great prowess. And although she fought with "so many proud and arrogant knights, and no one passing her with-"out giving her very heavy and vicious blows, yet she received them "all harmlessly upon her very hard and strong shield."

When two of the knights, Talanque and Maneli, saw what wonders the Queen was doing they attacked her with the greatest fury, as if they considered her absolutely insane. Seeing such an ungallant attack the Queen's sister Liota* rushed to her defence like a wild lioness, and fought the Caballeros so mortally that, to the loss of their honor, they were compelled to withdraw.

At this time the people of the fleets had the advantage, and had it not been for the mercy of God the city would have been taken.

The armies fought cruelly until nearly dark, and ten of the valiant 'Cruzados' had been killed in defending the gates. Both armies retired and Queen Calafia went to her fleet as her headquarters. Pages 242-3.

After these discomfitures the Queen Calafia was yet more anxious to obtain glory and fame if personal fighting would bring such comfort; so she joined the Sultan of Liguia in sending a challenge to Amadis and Esplandian.* It is a specimen pronunciamiento.

"Radiaro, Sultan of Liguia, shield and bulwark of the Turkish "law, destroyer of the Christians, cruel enemy of the enemies of the "gods; and the very mighty Queen Calafia, Señora of the great "island of California celebrated for its great abundance of gold and "the precious stones; do herewith declare to you Amadis de Gaula, "King of Great Britain, and to your son Knight of the Great Serpent, "that we have voluntarily come to these parts to destroy the City of "Constantinople, for the injuries and losses which the highly hon-"ored King Armato of Persia, our brother and friend, has received "from this wicked Emperor, giving him favor and aid because part "of his dominion had been seized by fraudulent means."

They announce their desire to gain fame, to have a fair combat, before the assembled armies, the conquered to submit to the will of the conquerors; and intimate that if the challenged do not accept, the Queen and her friend will count all the past glories of Amadis and Esplandian as belonging to the challengers.

---

*Is this from λεοντῆ, a lion's skin, or λέοντα, accusative singular of λέων, lion?

*Chapter CLXIV, page 545, column 1.

A "doncella negra y hermosa" richly attired and mounted upon a fiery horse, carried this challenge to the king and his son, who showed much courtesy to the doncella. After a very short consultation of the leaders King Amadis sent an acceptance, which permitted the challengers to use such arms as they thought proper.

When the negra hermosa returned to the Queen to report, she declared that all the Christian chieftains were beautiful, but the Knight of the Serpent exceeded any human being in majesty and beauty. This so inflamed the Queen that she decided to go alone to the headquarters of the enemy to see and talk with Esplandian. She worried all night whether to go armed or to appear simply as a woman. She decided on the latter course and in the morning dressed herself in the richest robes covered with gold and precious stones.

The animal which she rode never had a counterpart, except in the imagination of Elisabat or Doré. "They brought it out and she "mounted and set forth upon an animal more marvellous than had "ever been seen. It had ears shaped like two oval shields, in the "broad forehead was fixed but one eye that shone as a mirror. The "openings of the nostrils were very large, his beak short and quite "blunt, so that nobody could break it. From its mouth two tusks "stood up, each more than two palms in length. The color of the "body was golden, and was covered with many violet spots as those "on the ounce. It was larger than a dromedary, and had its hoofs "cloven like an ox. It ran as swiftly as the wind and leaped lightly "among the craggy rocks, holding itself erect in any place as well as "a mountain goat. Its food was dates, figs and raisins, and noth-"ing else. She was very beautiful, hind quarters, flank and fore-"quarters."*

The Queen had twenty of her most beautiful maids with her, mounted, and having trains four arms' length trailing on the ground, and had two thousand following. She saw the emperor and all the kings; she was struck with the beauty of Esplandian, and proposed to test his courage in a combat where she would confront Amadis, his father. If she and the Sultan conquered she proposed to have a private talk with this Knight of the Great Serpent.

In due time the terms were amicably arranged, the armies were drawn up opposite to each other, and the combat took place between them.

---

*Chapter CLXV, page 547.

The King Amadis and Esplandian being both armed in expecta-
tion of the coming of the Grand Radiaro, Sultan of Liguia, and of
Calafia, the Queen of California, waited but a short time when they
saw them approaching prepared for the combat. All the staff of the
leaders were present; and the people from the city. The walls and
towers were covered with people. The Emperor was present near
the scene and close to the wall. He commanded his daughter, the
beautiful Leonorina, attended by her duenas and maids of honor, to
occupy one of the towers that they might be able to see what her
caballero would do.

All on both sides were armed lest they might be betrayed,
and thus lose their rights. The King Amadis and his son [Esplan-
dian] were mounted upon handsome horses, and bearing their shields
helmets and lances, marched slowly before the beholders, and presented such a splendid appearance, that every one was struck
with astonishment at the wonderful sight.

The Sultan exclaimed in a loud voice: "Caballeros! does it please
you to discuss this matter before we begin the combat?" Amadis
did not respond until he had come close to them, when he said:

"Sultan! what do you wish?' 'That which I ask' said he, 'is that
"whoever is overcome if not dead, shall be prisoner, and taken by
"the victor without shackles.' 'I agree to your proposition,' said
"Amadis. 'Well, then,' announced the Sultan, 'let the combat
"begin!'

"They separated a short space, and the combat began. The
"Sultan encountered Esplandian on the shield with a great blow,
"and a piece of the lance passed him within an arm's length, but
"every one thought it had pierced his body; but it was not so, for
"the lance passed between the arm and the body without touching
"either. And Esplandian looking towards his beloved wife, struck
"the Sultan's shield and the iron passing through, turned its point
"on his armor. He was brought up so abruptly by the force of the
"encounter that he was thrown from his saddle to the ground. He
"raised his helmet and looking extremely handsome, passed by as if
"he had received no injury.

"The Queen then advanced toward Amadis, and he moved for-
"ward to meet her. Before they encountered she turned the butt
"end of her lance to the front and struck his shield in that manner
"with such force that the lance was broken to pieces, and that of

"Amadis missed the Queen; and they crashed together so furiously
"with their shields that by the great force of the collision the Queen
"was stunned and fell to the ground; and Amadis, with the head of
"his horse split in twain, fell with one of his legs under its body.
"When his son [Esplandian] saw this he leaped from his horse to the
"succor of his father in that dangerous position. In the mean-
"while the Queen recovering herself, put her hand on her sword, and
"joined the Sultan notwithstanding the extreme pain she suffered
"from the fall, and with her helmet on, and sword in hand, she very
"bravely renewed the assault. And Esplandian standing in full
"view of the adorable princess, whom he loved more than the
"Queen, gave so many hard blows to the Sultan who was losing the
"field, although he was one of the bravest among the pagans, and by
"his prowess had gained many great battles from his dexterity in the
"arts of war, but was now so disheartened because his blows seemed
"to have no force, that he was losing the battle. The Queen and
"Amadis now confronted each other, and she began to deal him very
"heavy blows; some he received on his shield, others he avoided;
"and as he would not put his hand upon his sword he seized a piece
"of her broken lance and struck her such heavy blows on the hel-
"met, that in a short time she was stunned and fell to the ground.

"When she saw this, she exclaimed: 'How is it, Amadis, that you
"think so little of my courage that you try to conquer me with a
"club?' And he answered: 'Queen, I have always been accus-
"tomed to serve and succor women, but you have taken up arms,
"and you deserve to lose everything you ever gained.' Then the
"Queen said to him: 'In what relation do you hold me? Now take
"the consequences.' And swinging her sword with both hands she
"struck at him with mighty rage. Amadis raised his shield, and on
"it received the blow which was given with such terrific force that
"the shield was broken in two pieces, one of which fell to the ground;
"and when he saw that she pressed him so closely, he shifted the
"broken lance to his left hand, grasped the rim of her shield with his
"right, and pulled her with so much force that he broke the
"strong cords with which it was fastened to her arm. He tore it
"from her, and holding it with one hand, he forced her down with one
"knee upon the ground, from which she rose so quickly that Amadis
"had to throw away his half shield, seize the other part, and grasp-
"ing the club stood before her, and demanded: 'Queen, yield as my

"prisoner, now that your Sultan has been conquered.' She turned her
"head and seeing that Esplandian had subdued the Sultan and held
"him as his prisoner, said: 'I beg to try my fortune once more.'
"Then she raised her sword with both hands above her head, and
"attempted to strike the crest of his helmet, believing she could
"cleave his head in two. But Amadis was very agile and side-
"stepped, so that the blow was averted; then he dealt her, with the
"fragment of his lance, such a vigorous blow upon the crest of her
"helmet, that it stunned her, and the sword fell from her hands.
"Amadis seized it, and as he saw her thus disabled he tugged at her
"helmet so viciously that he tore it from her head, and exclaimed,
" 'will you be my prisoner now?'
    " 'Yes,' she said, 'there is nothing else for me to do.' "

We need not continue the long drawn out story, except to say
that at this point Esplandian brought the Sultan forward, and the
four combatants moved on to the Royal Encampment.

The prisoners were given to the Infanta Leonorina; Queen Calafia
of California praised the handsome Esplandian to her face, and un-
blushingly exalted that of the Infanta. Compliments were ex-
changed. Of course, Calafia fell in love with Esplandian, but did
not make it known. However, when he was married to the Infanta
the Queen unburdened her heart to him as the new Emperor, who
gallantly gave her his cousin Talanque for a husband; and to the
Queen's sister, Liota, Talanque gave his younger brother, Maneli.

.   After the marriage ceremonies were performed according to Christian rites, the two fleets were joined; the Amazons became Christians; the Turks were beaten; and the fleets won much glory.

"Reina Calafia, mi buena amiga," transferred the island of California with all its gold and precious stones to her new allies, and it remained unmentioned until Fernando Cortés rediscovered it on this
western coast.

APPENDIX.

Bernal Diaz del Castillo was born at Medina del Campo in old Castile, about 1498, but the date of his death in Guatemala is not known; it was before 1593. Of humble birth, he determined to try his fortune in the New World. As a common soldier he served with Córdoba, and Grijalva, and finally with Cortés. He was in one hundred and nineteen battles, and present at the siege and capture of the City of Mexico in 1521. After returning from Honduras with his chief he settled as a planter. In 1568 he was regidor of the city of Guatemala; and was then engaged in writing his personal history. After reading the "Crónica de la Nueva España", by Gomara, 1554, he determined to expand the scope of his writing to the "Historia Verdadera de la Conquista de la Nueva España." The manuscript remained in a private library for fifty years, and was finally published in Madrid in 1632, by Father Remon, who appreciated its value.

Maurice Keating published an English translation in London, 1800; small quarto, 514 pages; but it omits much of the less important details. Our historian of Spanish discoveries and exploits in North and South America, W. H. Prescott, was charmed with the inherent truthfulness of Bernal Diaz. In 1837 a "Nueva Edicion Corregida," was published in Paris, in four duodecimo volumes containing 1630 pages, no authority given, only "Paris, Libreria de Rosa." The latest translation is by José Maria de Heredia, (1842-1905), whose annotations gave him a reputation for acute and scrupulous research and the intelligent application thereof. He was born at Fortuna-Cafeyere, near Santiago de Cuba, but received his education in France and made Paris his home, and acquired deserved repute.

INDEX

Amadis de Gaula, romance, Ticknor on, 21, 25; author, date, 25; translated, 24; Montalvo's version, 25; Cervantes on, 26; known to Bernal Diaz, 27.

Amadis de Gaula, character in Las Sergas de Esplandian, 40 ff.

Amazons, in antiquity, 28; in America, 28 f; mentioned by Columbus, 29; Cortés, 28, 30; on Dourado's map, 29; on Guzman's expedition, 30; in South-America, 31; in Esplandian, 35 ff.

Anian, Strait of, 10.

Arroyo, Father, 6, 7.

Baegert, Father, 5.

Bancroft, H. H., 7, 17 n.

Bandelier, Gilded Man. 29 n.

Barrow, Arctic Voyages, 16 n.

Beechey, F. W., Capt., 6 f.

Bisselius, Joannes, 3, 13, 31.

Borysthenes, river, 22.

Burney, James, Capt., 6.

Cabrillo, Juan Rodriguez, 10, 19 f.

Calafera, island in Esplandian, 34,35.

Calafia, queen of island of California, 2, 21, 31; etymology, 34; in Esplandian, 35 ff.

Califan, place mentioned in Amadis, 34.

Califeno, character in Esplandian, 34.

California, in early authorities, 3 ff, 17 ff; on early maps, 9 ff; an island, 3, 4, 9, 18; shown as island on maps, 12, 13, 14 f; inhabited by Amazons, 8, 28, 29, 30; named Islas Carolinas, 5; a peninsula, 3, 5, 10; first believed peninsula, then island, 5; a bay, 8, 17.

California, Gulf of, 3, 19: Californiae sinus, 4, 12: G. della Callifornia, 12; Sea of Cortés, 9; Vermilion sea, mar bermeia, mar rojo, 3, 4, 14, 29; mare Californiae, 13.

California, Name, given at discovery, 5; by Cortés, 5, 6, 7, 8, 17, 19; in common use about 1585, 20; first applied to bay or anchorage, then extended 6, 8, 17, 18; first appearance on map, 9; first time in print, 17; variant spellings on early maps, 10, 11, 12; in plural, Californias, 5, 12; name found in Esplandian, Ticknor, 21; Hale, 22.

California, Name, Derivation of, from Caolis, 4; from calida and fornax, 5, 6, 7; rejected for several reasons, 5, 6; from caliente and fornalla, 8; from cala and fornix, 5; from colofon, 7; from Indian Kali-forno,

Tchalifalñi-al, 7; missionaries found no trace of name among natives, 5, 6; from cal y forno, 8; from Kalifat, 8; name taken from Esplandian, 21 f; derived by Hale from Calif, 22; by G. D. from Greek (kalos and ornis) 1, 33, 34.

California, Point of, 11, 12, 19.

California, First Vessel named, 16.

Cape (Cabo, Capo, C.) Blanco, 13, 14; California (Callifornia, Califormia, Californo) 10, 11, 12; Engaño, 9; de Fortun, 10; Mendocino, 10, 19, 20; San Lucas, 3, 5, 11, 12, 14; Santa Clara, 3.

Carvajal, Gaspar, 31.

Castillo, see Domingo.

Catalina Island, 14.

Cedros (Cerros) Island, 9, 18, 19.

Cervantes, 26.

Chino, Father, 5, 13.

Christy, Miller, 11.

Columbus, 29 f; 32.

Compoi, Guiseppe, 5.

Coronado Expedition, 10n ; 11, 12.

Cortés, 5, 6, 7, 8, 9, 17, 18, 19, 28, 30.

Cortés, Sea of, see California, Gulf of.

Dahlgren, E. W., 9.

Dampier's Voyages, 13.

Davidson, George, Identification of Drake's Anchorage, 3 n; Voyages on Northwest Coast of America, 10 n; 17 n; 19 n.

De' Giganti, island, 3.

D'Herbelay, paraphrased Esplandian, 22.

Diaz del Castillo, Bernal, 7, 17 f, 27, 46.

Domingo del Castillo, 9.

Drake, Francis, 11.

Dudley, Robert, 3, 12.

Elisabat, Gran Maestro, fictitious author of Esplandian, 33.

Esplandian, Las Sergas de, 8; discussed by Ticknor and Hale, 21; written by Montalvo as sequel to Amadis, 25, 33; ridiculed by Cervantes, 26; pretended Greek authorship, Elisabat, 1, 33; etymology of names in, 33f; modern Spanish edition, 33; translations from, 35 ff.

Esplandian, hero of romance, 41 ff.

Estotilandia, 3.

Farrellónes, river, 4.

Fernandez de Medrano, Sebastian, 13, 14, 15.

Ferrelo, Bartolomé, 10, 19, 20.

Gayangos, Pascual de, 26 n; 33 n.

Griffins, 31, 34; in Esplandian, 36 ff.

Guzman, Beltran de, 30.

Hakluyt, 11, 20.

Hale, Edw. Everett, 5; name California from Esplandian, 21; derivation from Calif, 22.

Herrera, Antonio, 10, 18, 19.

Hittell, Theo. H., S.

Hondius, Iodocus, 11, 12; Henricus, 12.

Horn, George, 4.

Islas Carolinas, name applied to California, 5.

Jansonio, Giovanni, 3.

King Peak, 10, 19.

Kino, Father, see Chino.

League, Spanish, length of, 15.

Liota, character in Esplandian, 2, 34, 41, 45; etymology, 41.

Lobeira, Vasco de, 25.

Lok, Michael, 11.

Lorenzana, Francisco Antonio, 9, 29.

Loreto, 8.

Magdalena Bay, 18.

Marcou, Jules, 7, 10.

M. L., of Fresno, 8.

Montalvo, Garcia Ordonez de, 8, 25, 33.

Montanus, Arnoldus, 13.

München Maps, 12, 29 n.

Nova Albion, 11.

Ortelius, Abraham, 10.

Pararos Island, 14.

Peter Martyr, 11.

Point (P., Punta, Punctum, etc.) Arena, 10, 19; Californiae, 11; della Callifornia, 12; Concepcion; S. Apolline, 14; of California, 19.

Preciado, Francisco, 17, 18.

Ramusio, Giovanni Battista, 17 n.

San Abad, bay, 18;
San Clement, island, 14.

San José del Cabo, 12.

San Lucas, port, 19. (See also under Cape.)

San Miguel, island, 10, 19.

Sandoval, Gonzales, 8, 28, 30.

Santa Barbara Channel, 10, 14, 19.

Santa Cruz, Alonzo de, 9.

Santa Cruz, island, 17; port, 19.

Santa Marina, bay, 18.

Silver Map of the World, 11.

Slevin, Thomas E., 7.

Southey, Robert, translated Amadis, 24.

Sutil y Mexicana expedition, 12.

Terrestrial Paradise, 32.

Ticknor, George, first notice of California in Esplandian, 21; on Romances, 24; on Esplandian, 21; on Amadis, 25,

Ulloa, Francisco, 5, 8, 9, 17, 18, 19.

Venegas, Miguel, 5, 6, 29 n.

Vermilion Sea, see California, gulf of.

Villa-Manrique, Marquis, 20.

Vizcaino, Sebastian, 12 .

Winship, George Parker, 10 n.

Wytfliet, 12.

EXPLANATORY NOTE.

A copy of the title page of the 1587 edition of Las Sergas de Esplandian has been attached to this paper to show the size of the book and the style of announcement. A few years since I obtained the negative from the copy of the volume in the Boston Public Library.

Failing eyesight has prevented my reading the foregoing paper to check errors.

To Professor E. G. Linsley of the University of California I am deeply indebted for his kindness in collating my notes of the Chart of 1541.

To Mr. Hugh Jeidell of San Francisco my thanks are due for his reading the last proof.

GEORGE DAVIDSON

San Francisco, Cal., May 9th, 1910.

F. F. PARTRIDGE Print, 136 Leidesdorff St., San Francisco

CPSIA information can be obtained
at www.ICGtesting.com
Printed in the USA
BVHW030048260820
587163BV00002B/137

9 789353 604370